new homeoffice design

daab

Los nuevos estilos de vida, desarrollados vertiginosamente durante el siglo XX, han sido la causa de la aparición de nuevos tipos de trabajo y del desarrollo de nuevas maneras de ejecutarlos. Todo ello ha impulsado un replanteamiento del hábitat doméstico con el fin de encontrar un espacio adecuado donde llevar a cabo estas nuevas actividades profesionales. En la actualidad, muchos hogares han acondicionado zonas de trabajo para economizar los gastos del *freelance* y esta nueva situación confiere la oportunidad de poder desarrollar la labor en un ambiente personalizado y con una estética afín que aportan una mayor comodidad al trabajador; asimismo, los horizontes abiertos por la tecnología han transformado el diseño de los tradicionales espacios laborales.

Les nouveaux styles de vie, en plein essor au cours du dernier XX siècle, sont à l'origine de nouveaux types de travail et du développement de nouvelles manières de réaliser cette activité professionnelle. Tout cela a incité à repenser l'habitat familial, dans le but de trouver un espace adéquat où réaliser ces nouvelles professions. Dans beaucoup de foyers d'aujourd'hui, des zones de travail ont été conditionnées pour économiser des frais lorsqu'on réalise des professions free lance, ce qui permet aussi de pouvoir travailler dans une ambiance personnalisée et avec une esthétique en affinité, aspects qui apportent plus de confort; les horizons ouverts par la technologie ont ainsi transformé le design des espaces de travail traditionnels.

I nuovi stili di vita cresciuti in modo vertiginoso durante il XX° sec., sono stati la causa dell'apparizione di nuove forme di lavoro e dello sviluppo di nuovi modi di realizzare l'attività lavorativa. Tutto ciò ha stimolato una nuova impostazione dell'habitat domestico, allo scopo di trovare uno spazio adeguato dove realizzare queste nuove professioni. In molte case attuali sono state predisposte aree di lavoro per ridurre le spese di attività professionali free lance, il che conferisce l'opportunità di poter lavorare in un ambiente personalizzato e con un'estetica affine, aspetti questi che apportano maggior comodità. Allo stesso modo, gli orizzonti aperti dalla tecnologia hanno trasformato la progettazione dei tradizionali spazi di lavoro.

Das 20. Jahrhundert mit seinen atemberaubenden Veränderungen in allen Bereichen hat neue Beschäftigungsfelder hervorgebracht, die mit neuen Arbeitsformen und neuen Lebensstilen einhergehen. Daher ist es nur konsequent, dass es auch zu einem Umdenken bei der Gestaltung des häuslichen Umfelds gekommen ist, um einen Raum zu schaffen, in dem diese neuen Berufe angemessen verwirklicht werden können. In vielen modernen Haushalten werden bequeme Arbeitsbereiche eingerichtet und nach Gesichtspunkten persönlicher Ästhetik individuell gestaltet, um den Free-Lancern ein Arbeiten in angenehmer Atmosphäre zu ermöglichen. Die heutigen technologischen Möglichkeiten haben den Designern dieser Arbeitsbereiche außerdem völlig neue Perspektiven eröffnet.

The rapid evolution of new kinds of lifestyles over the past 20th century have generated new working schemes and new ways of carrying out professional activities that have transformed the working area into an integral part of the domestic space. Freelance professionals often opt to establish their office at home for economic reasons, as well as for the opportunity to work within a personalized space that is both aesthetic and comfortable. New forms of technology have also played a role in transforming the appearance and design of traditional working spaces.

Andrezj Zarzycki | London, UK
Studio in the Country
South of France | 2002

Anne-Dore Schäfer | Berlin, Germany

Loft of Leonore Leonardy and Stefan Iglhaut

Berlin, Germany | 2004

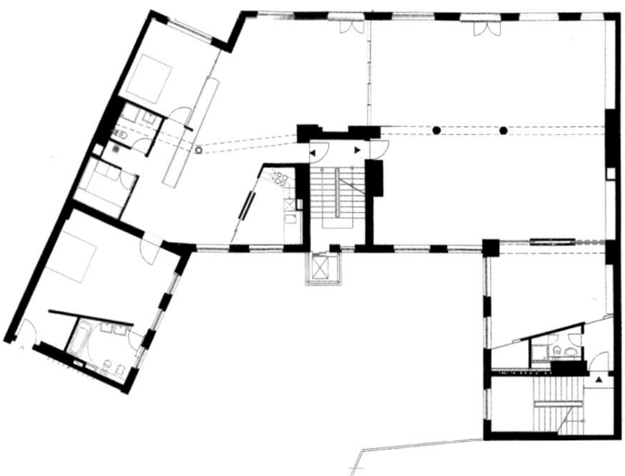

Arteks | Andorra la Vella, Principat d'Andorra

Penthouse in Andorra

Andorra la Vella, Principat d'Andorra | 2003

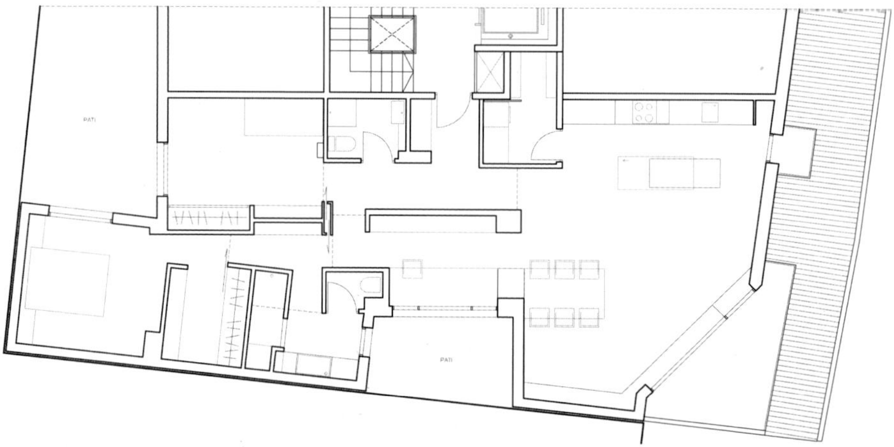

23 24 25 26 27 28 29
TUMBUKTU

TIBET

AV62 Arquitectos | Barcelona, Spain
D2 House
Bizkaia, Spain | 2002

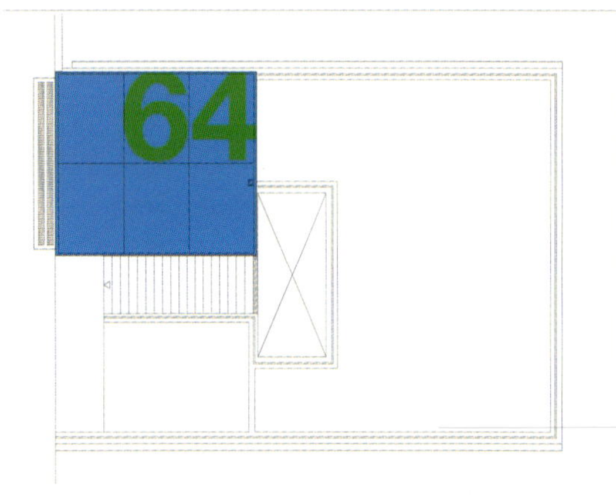

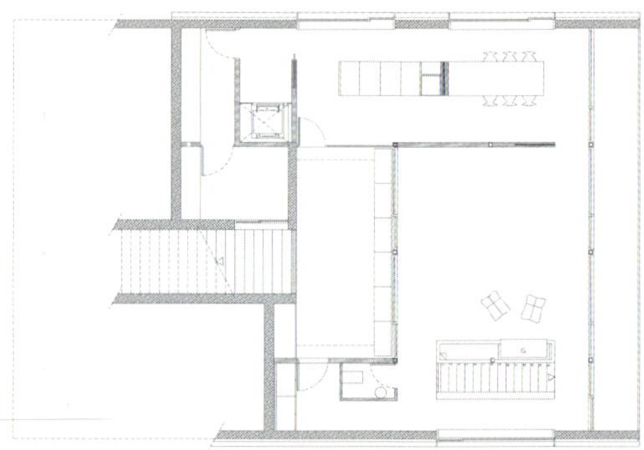

este jardín del que tanto

DOMENECH

Barwo Leibinger Architekten | Berlin, Germany

Renovated Apartment

Berlin, Germany | 2002

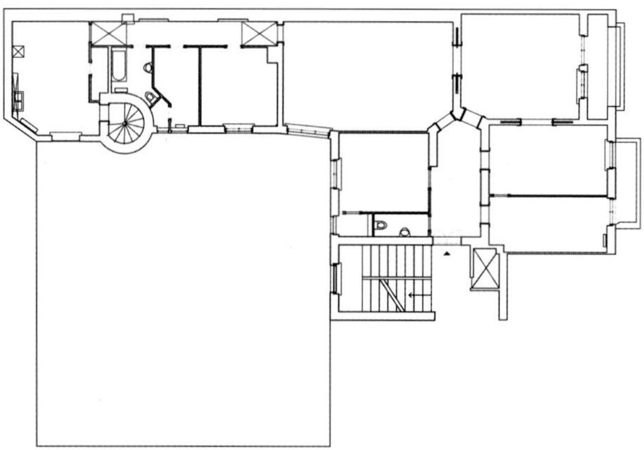

The Yale Shakespeare

PONS

Bluebase | London, UK

Loft in Charlotte Road

London, UK | 2002

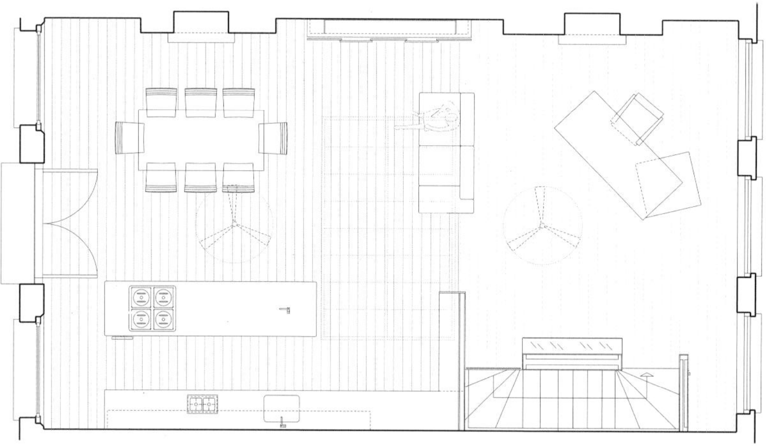

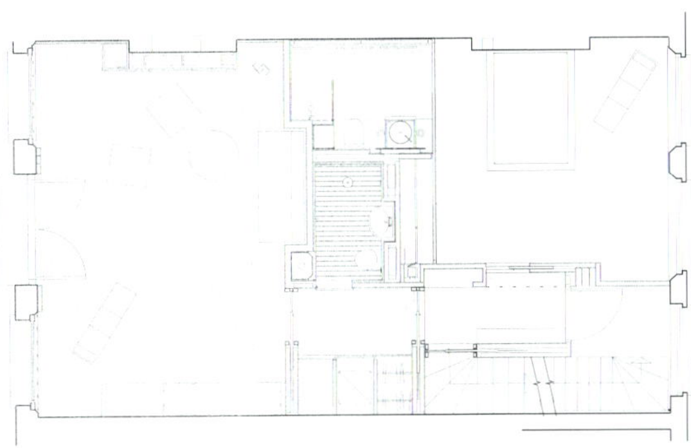

Carla Guerrini Architect | Prato, Italy

Studio in Prato

Prato, Italy | 2002

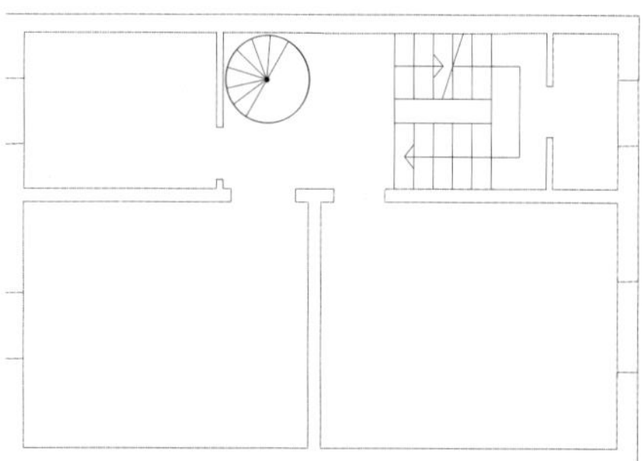

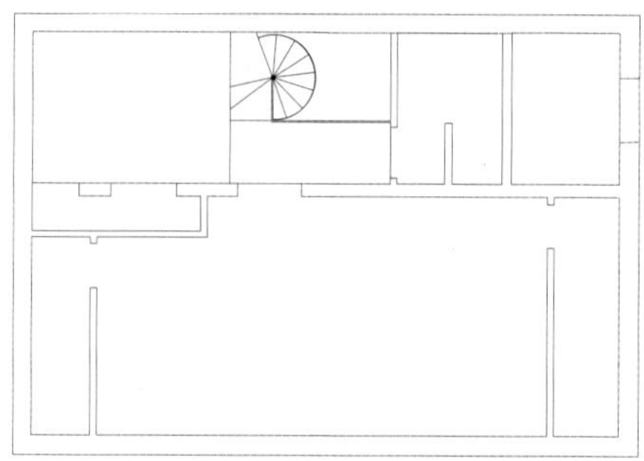

Carles Mir | Barcelona, Spain

White Serenity

Barcelona, Spain | 2003

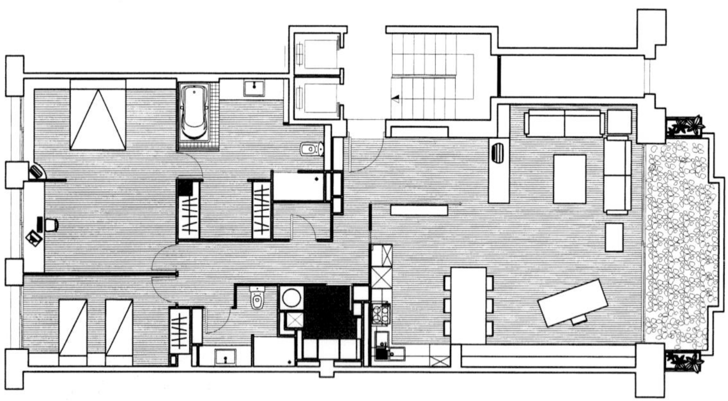

PUZZLE 1500

Cho Slade Architecture | New York, USA

Van Doren Apartment

New York, USA | 2003

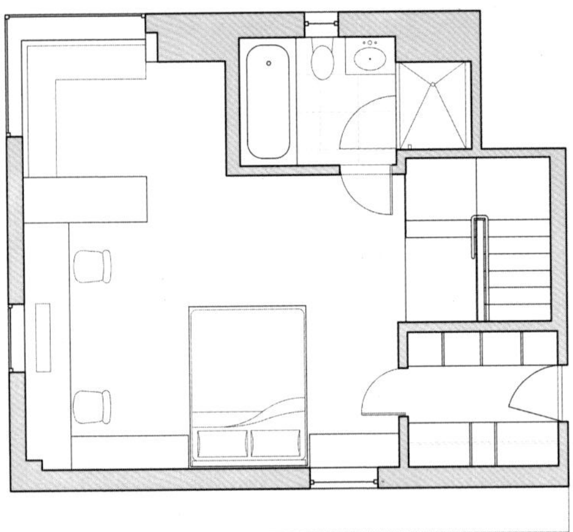

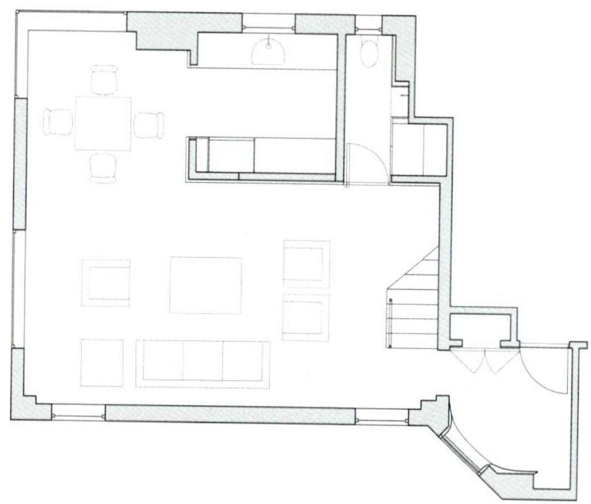

Cloud 9 / Enric Ruiz and Olga Subirós | Barcelona, Spain

Studio / Residence

Barcelona, Spain | 2003

BROSSA

THE HERMITAGE

David Salmela | Northwoods, Minnesota, USA

Ravenwood House

Northwoods, Minnesota, USA | 2001

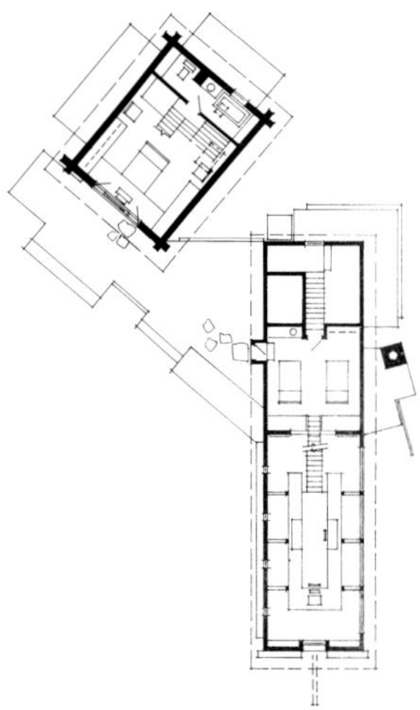

Elridge Smerin | London, UK
House in the Highgate Village
London, UK | 2003

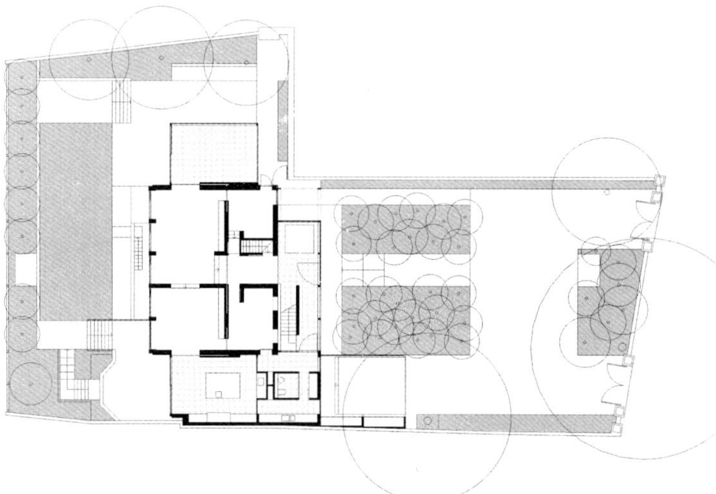

Estudio Farini.Bresnick | Madrid, Spain
Remodeled Penthouse
Madrid, Spain | 2003

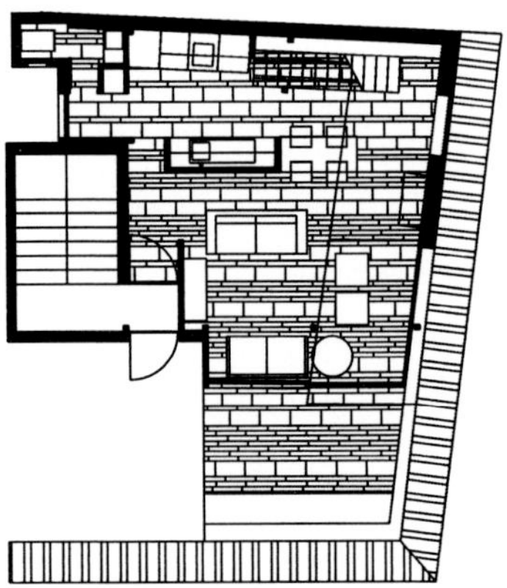

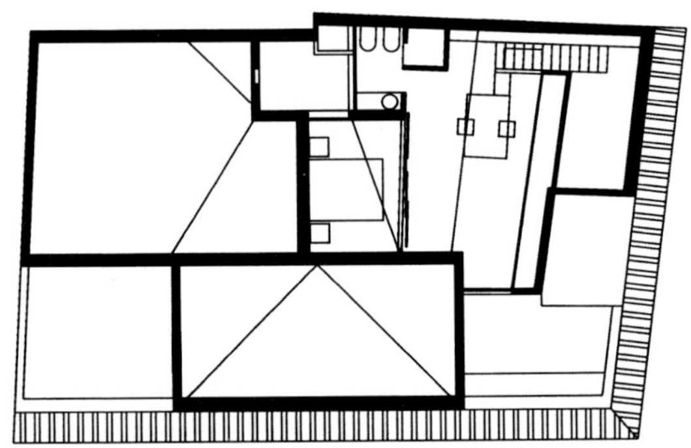

Felicity Bell | London, UK

Rosoman Street

London, UK | 2001

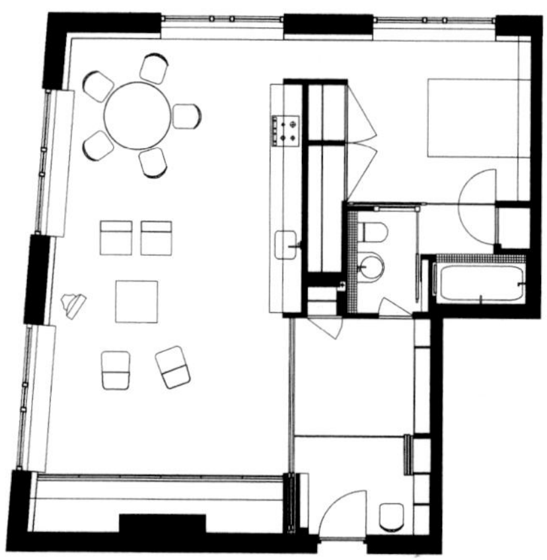

Feyferlik-Fritzer | Graz, Austria
Mariazell House
Graz, Austria | 2003

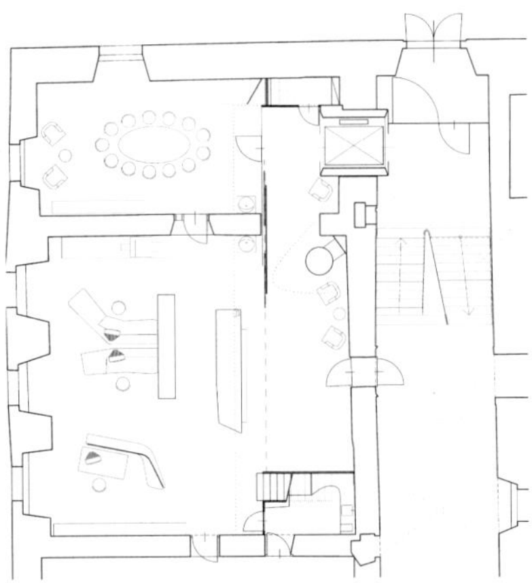

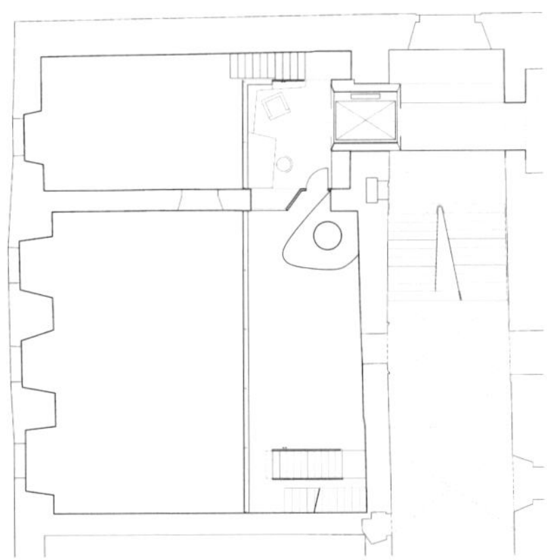

Florence Lim | London, UK
Florence Lim House
London, UK | 2002

Greek | Barcelona, Spain
House in Esplugues
Barcelona, Spain | 2004

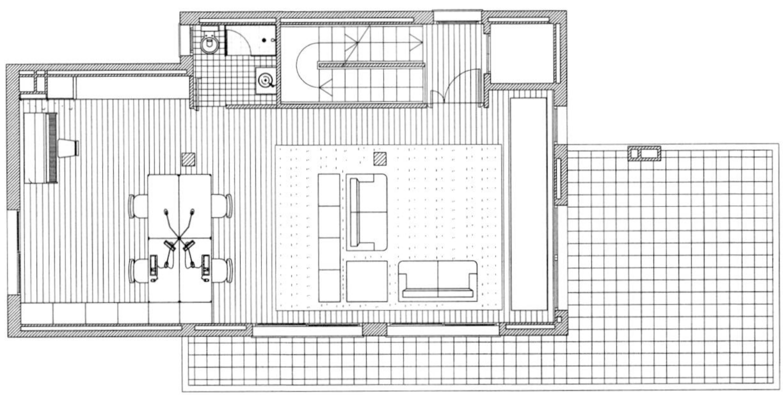

CASAS
DELL

Gustavo Barba | Barcelona, Spain
Architect's Home Office
Barcelona, Spain | 2004

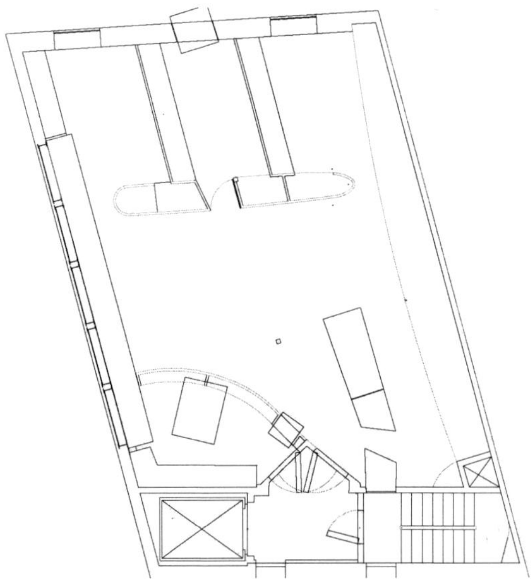

CATALUNYA DIA A DIA

Gustavo Barba | Barcelona, Spain

Flat in Fusina Street

Barcelona, Spain | 2003

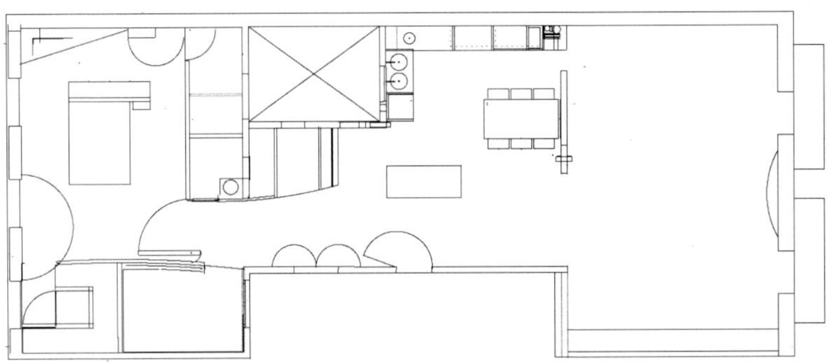

Miquel Barceló
HISTORIA DEL ARTE
PICASSO

Herzog & Partner | Munich, Germany

Residence near Paderborn

Munich, Germany | 2003

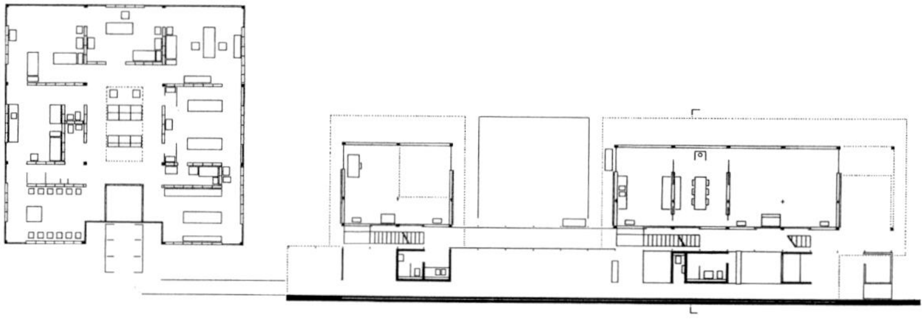

Juan Izquierdo | Madrid, Spain

Loft Palermo

Madrid, Spain | 2003

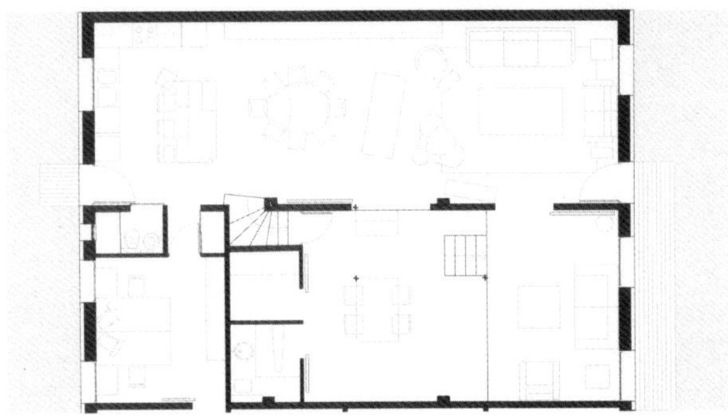

Klaus Wildner + Ulrico Falke | Borken, Germany

Wildner House

Borken, Germany | 2003

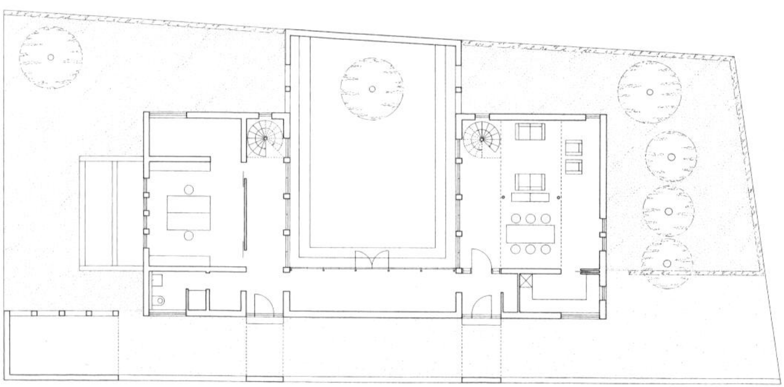

JOAN MIRO

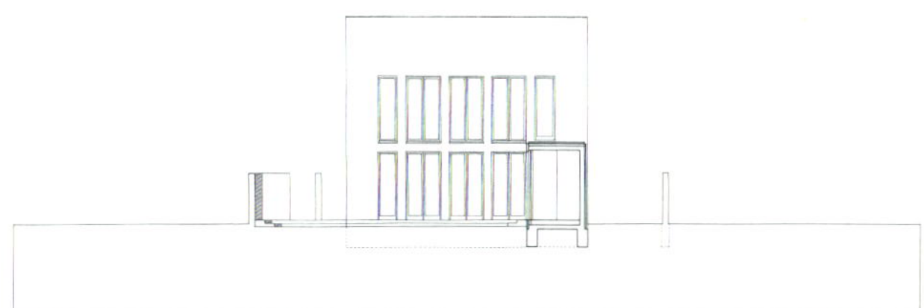

L.A. design & architecture studio / Leonardo Anneca, architect | Paris, France
Ministudio
Paris, France | 2004

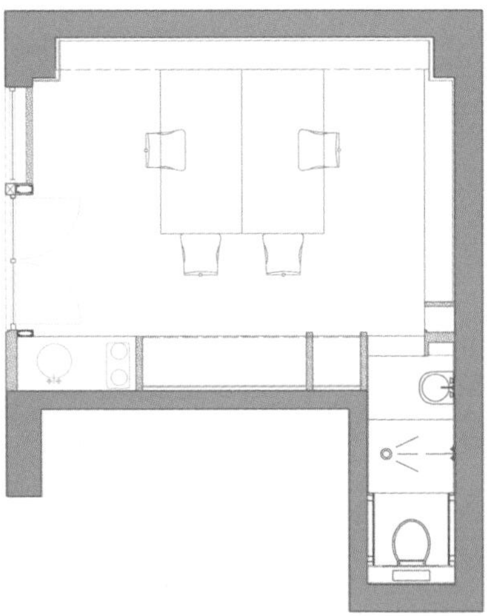

Word
Outlook
forster

INTERNI

Lehrer Architects | Los Angeles, USA
Architects' Office
Los Angeles, USA | 2000

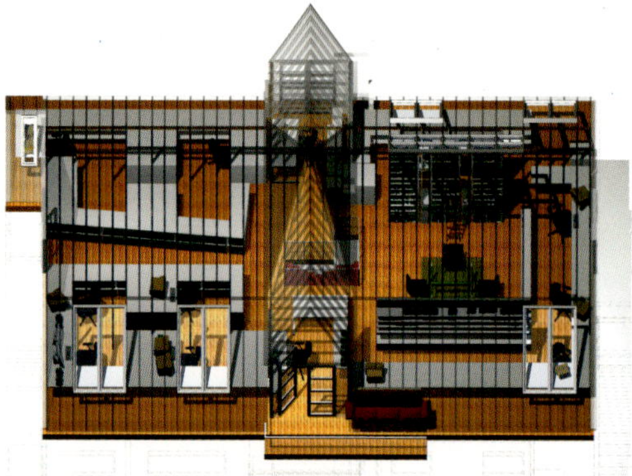

WATER
LIFE

lichtblau.wagner Architekten | Vienna, Austria
Apartment in Margareten
Vienna, Austria | 2001

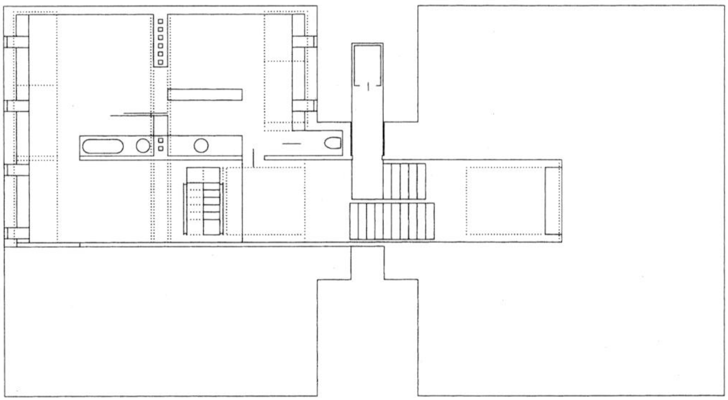

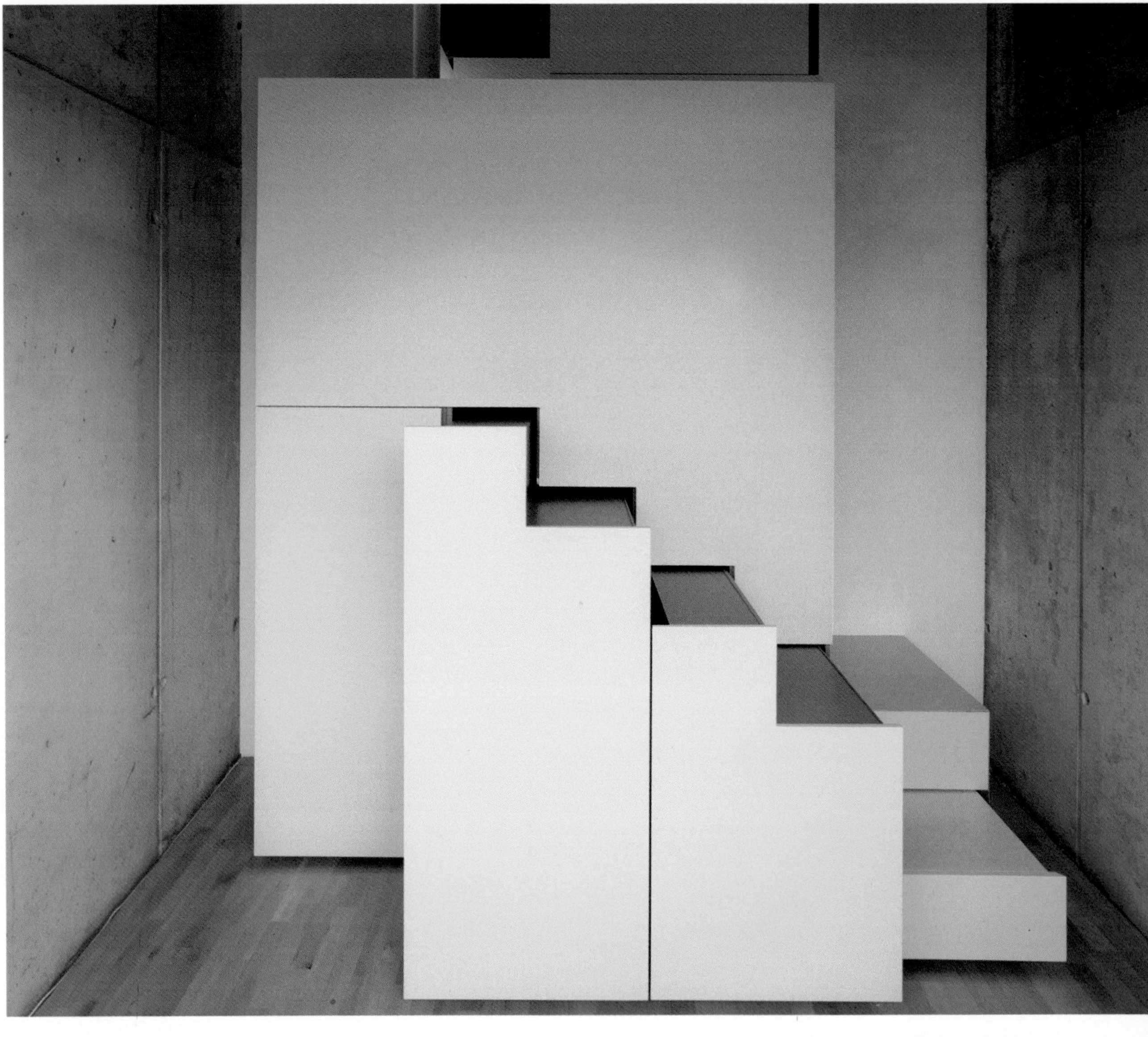

Lola Lago Interiores | Barcelona, Spain

Studio in San Cugat

Sant Cugat, Barcelona, Spain | 2004

sax
songs

Luccioni & Toraldo di Francia | Filotrano, Italy

Studio in Filotrano

Filotrano, Italy | 2002

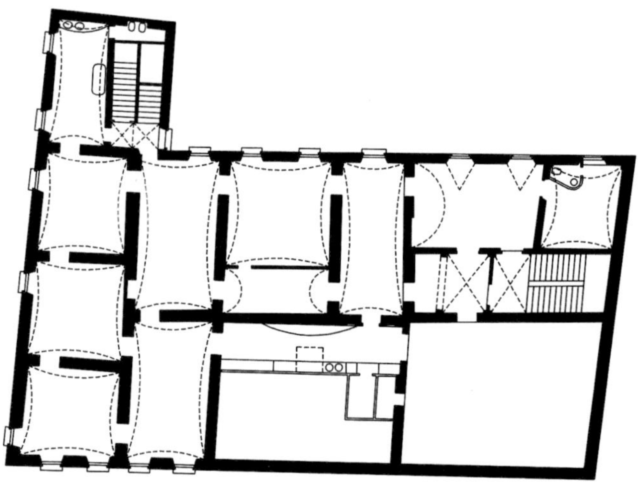

Memo Fisher | Bogotá, Colombia

Apartment in Bogotá

Bogotá, Colombia | 2003

NEW CLASSICISM
Architecture today

SPAIN

Minim | Barcelona, Spain

Open Mind

Barcelona, Spain | 2004

Nardi Architecture | Firenze, Italy
House in Firenze
Firenze, Italy | 2002

Moroccan Interiors

Oskar Leo Kaufmann | Vorarlberg, Austria

Innauer House

Dornbirn, Austria | 2002

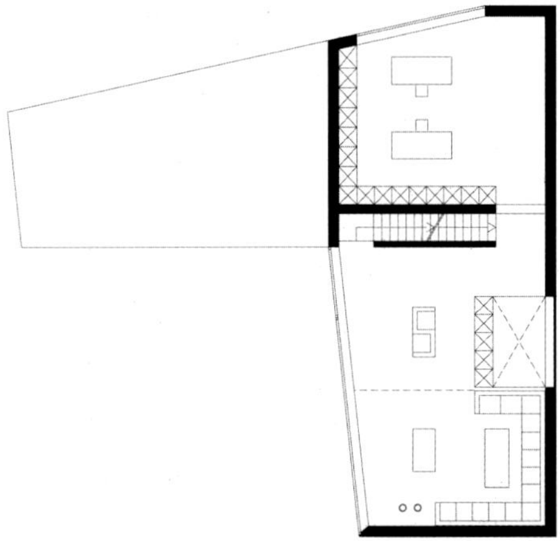

Pierre-François Caudoul Architecture at Associés | Paris, France

Apartment in Paris

Paris, France | 2002

Ricardo Flores and Eva Prats | Barcelona, Spain
Flat in l'Eixample
Barcelona, Spain | 2004

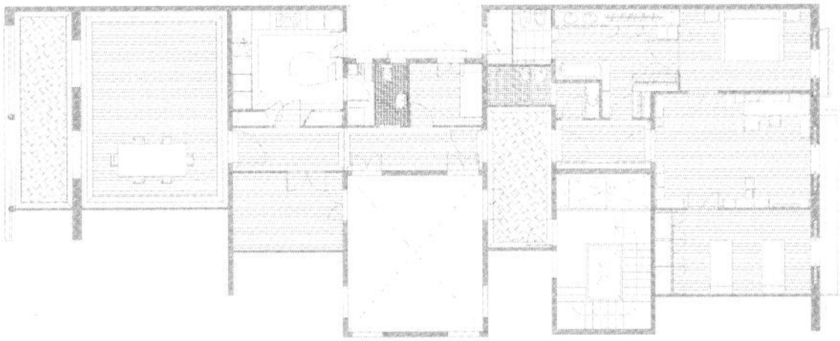

Roger Hirsch and Myriam Corti | New York, USA
Home for a Graphic Designer
New York, USA | 2002

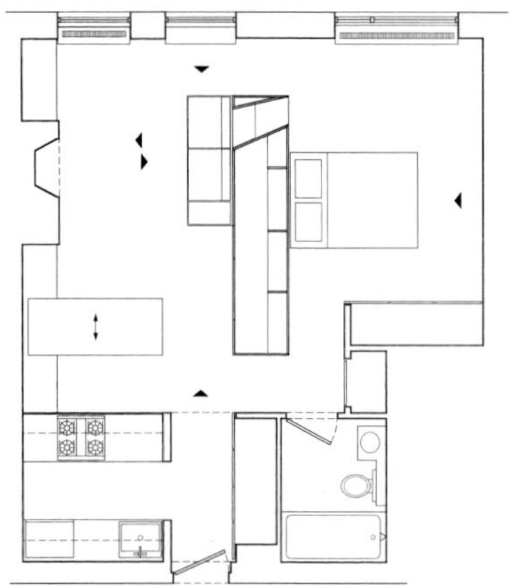

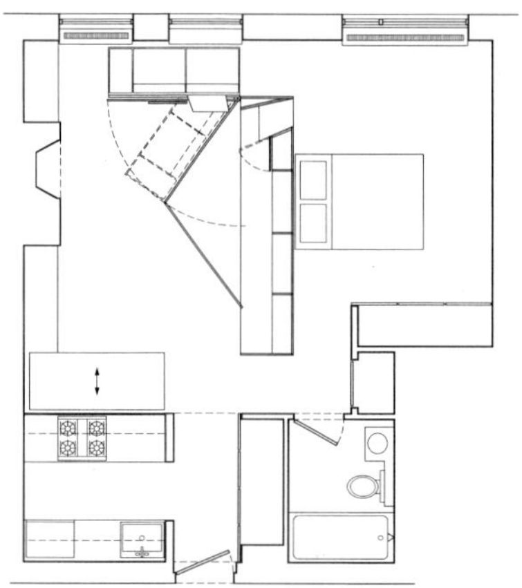

Integrated Solutions

advanced
1999 Goals
Integrated Solutions

Integrated Solutions
Our philosophy

Multiscan 500PS
SONY
BISLEY

Rulh Walker Architects | Boston, USA

Loft in Boston

Boston, USA | 2002

MAY
2001

COLLATERAL
EDI REPORT
FASHION REPORT

Sandra de Keller, designer | Barcelona, Spain
Man Without a Head
Barcelona, Spain | 2003

Paulo Coelho ● Der Fünfte Berg
23158
Juan Arias/Paulo Coelho ● Bekenntnisse eines Suchenden
23294
Paulo Coelho ● Am Ufer des Rio Piedra saß ich und weinte
23146
Paulo Coelho Der Dämon und Fräulein Prym
Paulo Coelho Handbuch des Kriegers des Lichts

Sara Colledge | London, UK
Flat in London
London, UK | 2002

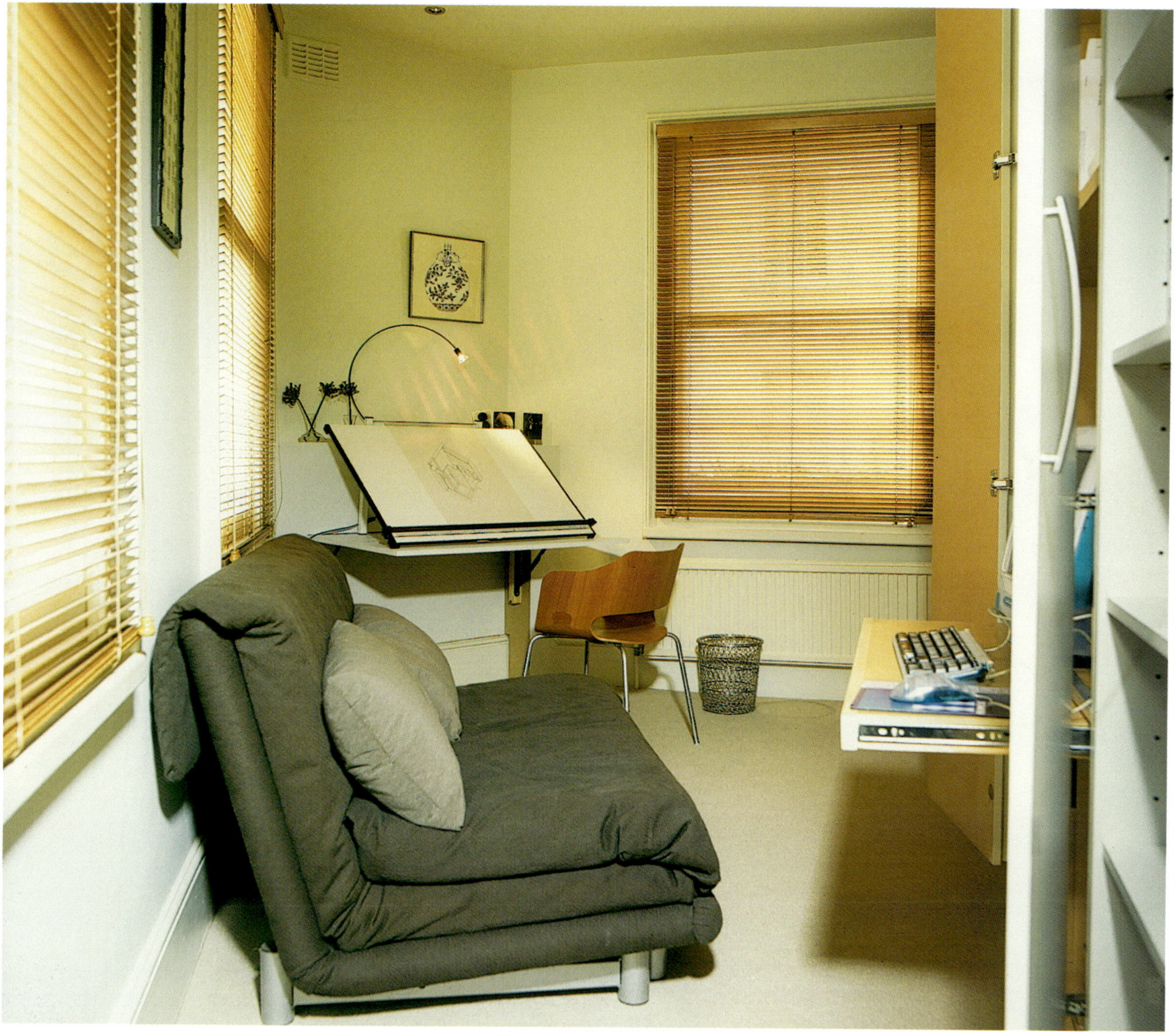

Sarah Folch Estudi d'Interiorisme | Barcelona, Spain
Loft in Passatge Sert
Barcelona, Spain | 2003

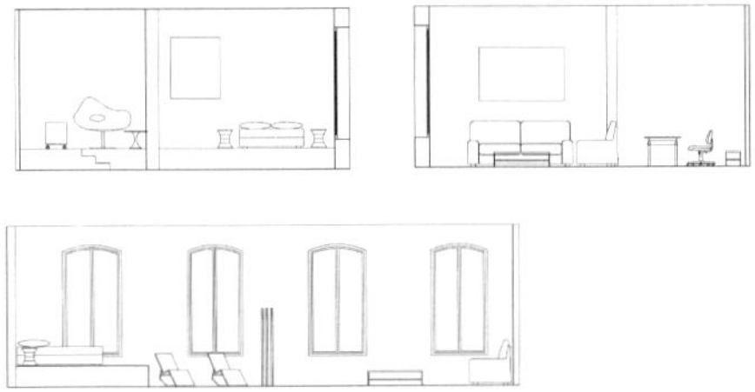

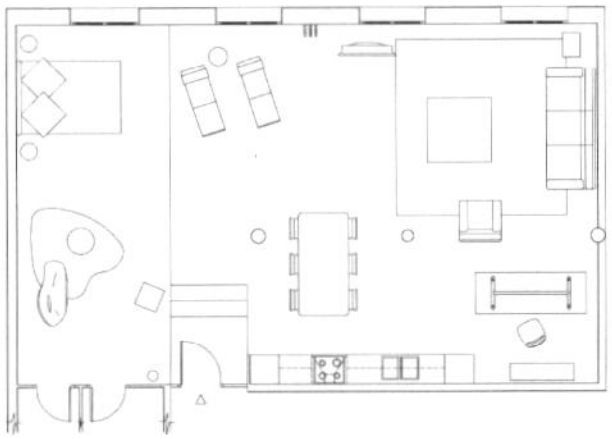

Tisettanta | Milan, Italy

Metropolis

Milan, Italy | 2004

11
III
MAR
ZO
MER
C'è posta per te !

Torsten Neeland, Industrial Design + Interior Design | London, UK
Robertson Apartment
London, UK | 2002

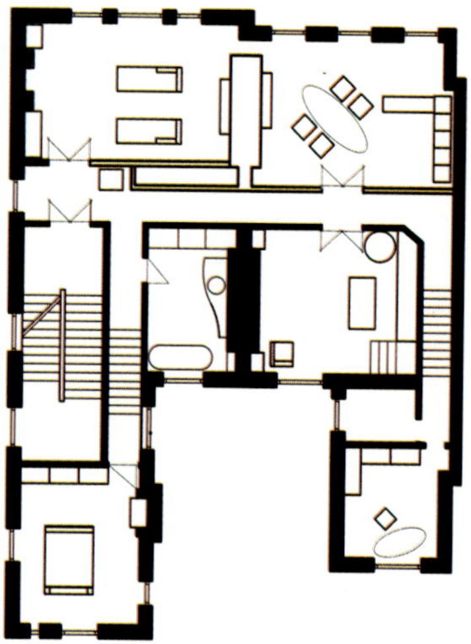

Vinçon | Barcelona, Spain

Small Studio

Barcelona, Spain | 2004

Travel Guru

Andrezj Zarzycki
London, UK
P +44 208 969 6967
F +44 208 960 6480
Studio in the Country
Photos: © Red Cover / Ken Hayden

Anne-Dore Schäfer
Taborstr. 4, 10997 Berlin, Germany
a.quatrat@snafu.de.
Loft of Leonore Leonardy and Stefan Iglhaut
Photos: © Wini Sulzbach

Arteks
C/ L'aigüeta 12, 1°, Andorra la Vella, Principat d'Andorra
P +376 823 202
F +376 823 272
arteks@andorra.ad
Penthouse in Andorra
Photos: © Eugeni Pons

AV62 Arquitectos
C/ Girona 62, Bajos derecha, 08009 Barcelona, Spain
P +34 93 231 22 66
F +34 93 231 37 34
www.av62arquitectos.com
info@av62arquitectos.com
D2 House
Photos: © Eugeni Pons

Barkow Leibinger Architekten
Schillerstrasse 94, 10625 Berlin, Germany
P +49 (0) 30 315712 0
F +49 (0) 30 315712 29
www.barkowleibinger.com
Renovated Apartment
Photos: © Werner Huthmacher

Bluebase
56 Clerkenwell Road, GB London, EC1M 5PX, UK
P +44 (020) 7253 8284
F +44 (020) 7253 8280
www.bluebase.com
info@bluebase.com
Loft in Charlotte Road
Photos: © View / Peter Cook

Carla Guerrini Architect
Via del Palco 16, 59100 Prato, Italy
P/F +39 0574 607 480
c.guerrini@comune.fi.it
Studio in Prato
Photos: © Alessandro Ciampi

Carlos Mir
C/ Marqués de Monistrol 17, 08960 Barcelona, Spain
P +34 934 733 124
F +34 934 700 629
carlosmir@retemail.es
White Serenity
Photos: © Montse Garriga

Cho Slade Architecture
367 East 10th St, New York, NY 1009, USA
P +01 212 677 6380
F +01 212 677 6330
www.sladearch.com
Van Doren Apartment
Photos: © Jordi Miralles

Cloud 9 / Enric Ruiz and Olga Subirós
Passatge Mercader 10, 08008 Barcelona, Spain
P +34 93 215 05 53
www.e-cloud9.com
Studio / Residence
Photos: © Luis Ros

David Salmela
Northwoods, Minnesota, USA
Ravenwood House
Photos: © Peter Kerze

Elridge Smerin
17, Cinnamon Row, Plantation Wharf, London SW11 3TW, UK
P +44 (020) 722 82824
F +44 (020) 722 82825
www.eldridgesmerin.com
mail@eldridgesmerin.com
House in the Highgate Village
Photos: © View / Chris Gascoigne

Estudio Farini.Bresnick
C/ Piamonte 7, 28004 Madrid, Spain
P/F +34 91 319 19 32
estudiofb@arquired.es
Remodeled Penthouse
Photos: © Eugeni Pons

Felicity Bell
63-67 Rosoman Street, London EC1R 0HY, UK
P + 44 (0)20 7689 0213
F + 44 (0)20 7713 6759
studio@felicitybell.com
Rosoman Street
Photos: © Chris Tubbs

Feyferlik-Fritzer
Glacisstraße 7, 8010 Graz, Austria
P +43 316 347 656
F +43 316 382 960
feyferlik@inode.at
fritzer@inode.cc
Mariazell House
Photos: © Paul Ott

Florence Lim
London, UK
Florence Lim House
Photos: © Red Cover/Henry Wilson

Greek
C/ Rubinstein 4, 08022 Barcelona, Spain
P +34 93 418 95 50
F +34 93 418 95 32
www.greekbcn.com
House in Esplugues
Photos: © Nuria Fuentes

Gustavo Barba
Antic de Sant Joan 12, 2ª, 08003 Barcelona, Spain
P +34 93 268 21 03
arteks@andorra.ad
Architect's Home Office
Photos: © Nuria Fuentes
Flat in Fusina Street
Photos: © Nuria Fuentes

Herzog & Partner
Imhoftrasse 3A, 80805 Munich, Germany
P: +49 89 360 570
F: +49 89 360 571 39
Residence Near Paderborn
Photos: © Artur / Dieter Leistner

Juan Izquierdo
C/ Palermo 19, Bajo interior, 28043 Madrid, Spain
P +34 91 759 00 22
F +34 91 300 08 75
geniusloci@retemail.es
Loft Palermo
Photos: © Eugeni Pons

Klaus Wildner + Ulrich Falke
Graf-Herman-Otto-Weg 10
D-46325 Borken, Germany
P +49 2861 602390
F +49 2861 602391
wildner-falke@t-online.de
Wildner House
Photos: © Werner Huthmacher

L.A. design & architecture studio / Leonardo Anneca, architect
53, Rue Montreuil, 75011 Paris, France
P +33 (0) 1 444 99006
www.l-a-design.com
press-director@l-a-design.com
Ministudio
Photos: © Happyliving.dk

Lehrer Architects
2227 Talmadge Street, Los Angeles, CA 90027, USA
P 323 664 4747
F 323 664 3566
www.lehrerarchitects.com
Architect's Office
Photos: © Michael B. Lehrer

lichtblau.wagner Architekten
Diehlgasse, 50/17 18, A-1050 Vienna, Austria
P +43 1 545 18 54-0
F +43 1 545 18 54-4
www.lichtblauwagner.com
office@lichtblauwagner.com
Apartment in Margareten
Photos: © Bruno Klomfar

Lola Lago Interiores
C/ Balmes 5, 08193 Bellaterra, Barcelona, Spain
P +34 93 580 79 68
F +34 93 580 19 74
www.lolalagointeriores.com
Studio in Sant Cugat
Photos: © Eugeni Pons

Luccioni & Toraldo di Francia
Via Rosselli 12, 60024 Filotrano (AN), Italy
P +39 0717 220 974
F +39 0717 222 978
luccioni@marcheonline.net
toraldo@marcheonline.net
Studio in Filotrano
Photos: © Alessandro Ciampi

Memo Fisher
Calle 80, 5-02, Apt. 501, Bogotá, Colombia
P +57 1 636 24 84
F +57 1 636 29 95
gfisher@col.net.co
Apartment in Bogotá
Photos: © Alejandro Bahamón

Minim
Av. Diagonal 369, 08037 Barcelona, Spain
P +34 93 272 24 25
F +34 93 488 34 47
www.minim.es
info@minim.es
Open Mind
Photos: © Nuria Fuentes

Nardi Architecture
Firenze, Italy
House in Firenze
Photos: © G. Bouchet / A. Cardinale

Oskar Leo Kaufmann
Steinebach 3, 6850 Dornbirn, Vorarlberg, Austria
P +43 (0) 5572 / 39 4969
www.olk.cc
office@olk.cc
Innauer House
Photos: © Adolf Bereuter

Pierre-François Caudoul Architecture et Associés
Paris, France
P +33 613 23 83 49
Apartment in Paris
Photos: © Omnia / Philippe Ruault

Ricardo Flores and Eva Prats
C/ Trafalgar 12, 3°1ª, Barcelona 08010, Spain
P +34 93 268 46 35
F +34 93 268 29 51
flores.prats@coac.net
Flat in l'Eixample
Photos: © Eugeni Pons

Roger Hirsch and Myriam Corti
91 Crosby Street, New York, NY 10012, USA
P +1 212 219 26 09
www.rogerhirsch.com
Home for a Graphic Designer
Photos: © Minh+Wass

Rulh Walker Architects
60K Street, Boston, MA 02127, USA
P +01 617 268 5479
F +01 617 268 5488
www.rulhwalker.com
Loft in Boston
Photos: © Jordi Miralles

Sandra de Keller, designer
c/ Aribau 252, 1°1ª, 08006 Barcelona, Spain
P +34 606 04 24 45
cyclopictures@hotmail.com
Man Without a Head
Photos: © Conrad White

Sara Colledge
London, UK
Flat in London
Photos: © Red Cover / Guglielmo Galvin

Sarah Folch Estudi d'Interiorisme
Plaça Sarrià 12, 2°1ª, 08017 Barcelona, Spain
P +34 93 280 04 28
sarafolch@yahoo.es
Loft in Passatge Sert
Photos: © Jordi Miralles

Tisettanta
Via Tofane 37, I-20034 Giussano, Milan, Italy
P +39 0362 31 91
F +39 0362 31 93
www.tisettanta.com
info@tisettanta.it
Metropolis
Photos: © Tisettanta

Torsten Neeland, Industrial Design + Interior Design
61 Redchurch Street, London, E2 7DJ, UK
P +44 (0) 77 29 65 47
F +44 (0) 7366 65 33
tn@torsten-neeland.co.uk
www.torsten-neeland.co.uk
Robertson Apartment
Photos: © Christoph Kicherer, © Zapaimages/Bruno Helbling

Vinçon
Passeig de Gràcia 96, 08008 Barcelona, Spain
P +34 93 215 60 50
www.vincon.com
bcn@vincon.com
Small Studio
Photos: © Nuria Fuentes

published and distributed worldwide by
daab gmbh
stadtwaldgürtel 57
d - 50935 köln

t +49-221-94 10 740
f +49-221-94 10 741

mail@daab-online.de
www.daab-online.de

publisher ralf daab
rdaab@daab-online.de

art director feyyaz
mail@feyyaz.com

editorial project by loft publications

editor Encarna Castillo
layout Emma Termes
english translation Ana Cristina G. Cañizares
french translation Jean Pierre Layre Cassou
italian translation Grazia Suffritti
german translation Martin Fischer
copy editing Raquel Vicente Durán

printed in spain
Anman Gràfiques del Vallès, Spain
www.anman.com

isbn 3-937718-12-5
d.l.: B-27623-2004